Dear, Elijah,

You Are Worthy Of Love.

Candide Uwizeyimana

Amazon Book Publishing Center works with authors, and aspiring authors, who have a story to tell and a brand to build. Do you have a book idea you would like us to consider publishing?

Please visit amazonbookpublishingcenter.com for more information.

Acknowledgments

I thank many people who have contributed to my book throughout this journey. To Jeanine Takala for opening the doors for me, to my friend Stephanie Webb for her endless support, to my former foster parents who absolutely love and adore Elijah, to also thank Dr. Kim and the entire ECE Department at North Seattle for shaping me into a professional ECE advocate that I am.

But most importantly, I want to thank my son Elijah for being my biggest inspiration and transforming me into a fearless, creative, risk-taking, gentle, and loving mother to you. I would also like to thank my friend for carrying out my project and sharing it on different platforms.

Dear Elijah, you are worthy of love.

I think of you when we are apart as well as when we are together. Your bright and beautiful smile and gentle touches make me smile.

Having you put everything in perspective, and everything else disappeared. From your heartbeats to you laying on my chest for the first time, you made our home happier.

Days were shorter, and so were nights as I watched you fall asleep. Holding you in my arms so gently was the best. You are the best, chosen just for me.

My world is better, calmer, gentle, careful, thoughtful, and brighter with you in it.

Before I had you, I always wondered what a mother's warmth and love would feel like. And when you came into my life, everything changed for the best.

You were the best gift and surprise any mother can wish for.

For the last few years that you have been on this earth, we have experienced so much together.

You motivate me to wake up every morning, even when I am tired. Hearing you say, "Mama go, Elijah goes," I rise up stronger like never before.

You brought love around, and
the whole world couldn't wait to meet you!

Elijah, you are loved.
I will do my best to protect you and
keep you safe because you are worthy to be loved.

I have faith in you, and as you grow,
you will face challenges, but always know
that you can handle it.

Better is possible, and the secret to getting ahead in life is by getting started and working hard for what you want.

You will enjoy celebrating your own accomplishments as much as others, and that will motivate you to go on in life.

Most of all, always be yourself, you will discover that the best you of who you are is you that is and will always be.

Child of mine always be yourself and be proud of what makes you unique from others.

I encourage you to try to express yourself because those who love you will always listen, be there and will never judge you.

Promise me that you will remember that you are braver than you believe, stronger than you seem, smarter than you think, and unique to the world.

Don't hesitate to believe these truths even when it gets hard because one day you will be a man and a man will cry. That shows that you are brave.

You are braver than you think, and to be honest, follow your heart, which will lead you to your dream and don't be afraid to try new things. Don't forget to be silly, kind, and most importantly, honest and love yourself.

No matter how hard things have gotten as I figure out all about this motherhood, your presence in my life made the past forgotten, smooth, and the future worth living.

It's my heart where you belong, and each day,
I love you even more than you know. Remember
to come home where care and comfort lays.

To my child Elijah, there are a lot of people like you, but you will always be the only you.

About the Author:

My name is Candide Uwizeyimana, and I am thrilled to announce that I am now an author. My first self-published book is a dedication to my amazing Elijah. "You are Worthy of Love" is a children's book for ages 3+ and older. It will inspire children with the freedom to follow their most expansive dreams and create the loving and just world we all want to see. By highlighting the importance of loving, affirming, and nurturing our children, this book is relatable for everyone, including older children and mothers, parents, grandparents, and caregivers. My inspiration is to promote culturally affirming literacy and knowledge in the early stages of childhood as well as build this habit for parents like me.

Once the book is available for purchase, please support it with reviews and share this book with your communities.

~Candide~

www.ingramcontent.com/pod-product-compliance
Lightning Source LLC
Chambersburg PA
CBHW041132120626
46547CB00019B/2965